FAST FINGER SNACKS

Your Promise of Success

Welcome to the world of Confident Cooking, created for you in
the test kitchen, where recipes are double-tested by our team
of home economists to achieve a high standard of success.

MURDOCH BOOKS®
Sydney • London • Vancouver

Food to go

These recipes are designed with speed and convenience in mind. They're home-cooked fast food, which can be eaten without formality by people in a hurry. Perfect for substantial family snacks, many recipes can double as party food, specially suitable for young people with hearty appetites.

Tangy Tomato Dip with Pitta Crisps

Preparation time:
  15 minutes
Total cooking time:
  10 minutes
Makes 2 cups

2 tablespoons oil
1 onion, chopped
2 cloves garlic, crushed
2 small red chillies,
  chopped
425 g can tomatoes,
  crushed
2 pimientos, chopped
2 tablespoons lemon
  juice
1/3 cup chopped parsley
3 pitta bread pockets
1/4 cup sour cream

1. Preheat oven to moderate 180°C. Heat oil in a medium pan, add onion, garlic and chillies. Stir over medium heat for 2 minutes or until the onion is tender.
2. Add tomatoes, pimientos and lemon juice, bring to boil. Reduce heat to low and simmer uncovered for 5 minutes or until reduced and thickened. Stir in parsley.
3. Split pitta pockets in half, cut each into eight triangles. Place in single layer on oven tray. Bake 10 minutes or until golden brown and crisp.
4. Spoon dip into bowl, top with sour cream. Serve warm or cold, as a dip for pitta crisps.

Note: Pimientos are cooked capsicum, bought in jars. To cook your own, grill the capsicum until black, cool and peel off skin.

Tangy Tomato Dip with Pitta Crisps.

Devilled Chicken Wings

Preparation time:
5 minutes
Total cooking time:
45 minutes
Serves 4

1/3 cup tomato sauce
2 tablespoons French
  mustard
1 tablespoon
  worcestershire sauce
2 teaspoons dried
  oregano leaves
1 onion, finely chopped
2 cloves garlic,
  crushed
12 chicken wings

1. Preheat oven to moderately hot 210°C (190°C gas). Combine tomato sauce, mustard, worcestershire sauce, oregano, onion and garlic in a large baking dish. Add chicken wings, stir until chicken is well coated.
2. Bake for 45 minutes or until chicken is golden brown. Turn chicken occasionally and brush with mixture during cooking.

Variation: Use chicken drumsticks, if more convenient, but allow extra cooking time.

Crispy Samosas

Preparation time:
20 minutes
Total cooking time:
4 minutes each batch
Makes 16

2 sheets ready-rolled
  puff pastry
oil for deep-frying

Filling
200 g pork and veal
  mince
1 medium carrot, finely
  grated
1/2 cup frozen peas,
  thawed
2 cloves garlic, crushed
2 teaspoons curry
  powder
2 tablespoons tamarind
  sauce

1. Cut each pastry sheet into four squares. Cut each square into two triangles.
2. *To make Filling:* In a small bowl, combine mince, carrot, peas, garlic, curry powder and tamarind sauce.
3. Divide filling evenly between pastry triangles. Brush edges of pastry with a little water. Fold pastry over to enclose filling and form small triangles. Press edges together to seal.
4. Heat oil in deep heavy-based pan. Gently lower small batches of samosas into moderately hot oil. Cook over medium-high heat for 4 minutes or until golden and crisp and cooked through. Carefully remove from oil with tongs or slotted spoon. Drain on paper towel, keep warm. Repeat with remaining samosas. Serve with a bowl of chutney.

Note: Have the oil deep enough to allow the samosas to float.

HINT
Tamarind sauce has an acidic flavour. If you can't find it in the supermarket, try an Asian food shop. Cakes of tamarind pulp are also available, in plastic packets. These can be dissolved in hot water and strained. Lemon juice is a good substitute.

Devilled Chicken Wings (top) and Crispy Samosas.

Sesame Prawns with Tangy Mint Chutney

Preparation time:
  20 minutes
Total cooking time:
  2 minutes per batch
Serves 4

1 kg (about 24)
  uncooked large king
  prawns
1/4 cup plain flour
1 egg, lightly beaten
2/3 cup dried
  breadcrumbs
1/2 cup sesame
  seeds
oil for deep frying

Tangy Mint Chutney
1 cup fresh mint leaves,
  firmly packed
1/2 cup fruit chutney
2 tablespoons lemon
  juice

1. Peel prawns, leaving tails intact. Cut prawns down the back, devein, flatten prawns slightly.
2. Toss prawns in flour; shake off excess. Dip prawns in beaten egg, coat with combined breadcrumbs and sesame seeds.
3. Heat oil in a deep, heavy-based pan. Gently lower prawns into moderately hot oil. Cook over medium-high heat for 2 minutes or until golden brown. Carefully remove from oil with tongs or a slotted spoon. Drain on paper towel.
4. **To make Tangy Mint Chutney:** Combine mint, chutney and lemon juice in a blender or food processor bowl. Process for 15 seconds or until smooth. Serve as a dip for prawns.

Sesame Prawns with Tangy Mint Chutney.

Peel and devein prawns, leaving the tails intact. Flatten slightly.

Dip prawns into beaten egg, coat with combined breadcrumbs and seeds.

Cook *prawns in hot oil for 2 minutes or until golden brown.*

For *chutney, process mint, chutney and lemon juice until smooth.*

Beef Satay Skewers with Quick Peanut Sauce

Preparation time:
 15 minutes
Total cooking time:
 12 minutes
Serves 4

500 g rump steak
1 tablespoon oil
1 tablespoon honey
1 tablespoon soy
 sauce

Quick Peanut Sauce
1/2 cup peanut butter
1 tablespoon soy sauce
1/2 cup water
2 teaspoons sweet chilli
 sauce

1.Trim meat of excess fat and sinew; cut into thin strips. Thread meat onto eight short bamboo skewers. Combine oil, honey and soy sauce in a small bowl.
2. Place meat on lightly oiled grill tray; brush with oil mixture. Cook under medium heat for 12 minutes, brushing with oil mixture occasionally. Serve hot with peanut sauce.

3. *To make Quick Peanut Sauce:* Place peanut butter, soy sauce, water and chilli sauce in a small pan. Stir over medium heat until smooth.

Fetta Triangles

Preparation time:
 20 minutes
Total cooking time:
 25 minutes
Makes 8

2 teaspoons oil
1 small onion, finely
 chopped
6 (300 g) large
 silverbeet leaves
1/2 cup grated cheddar
 cheese
140 g fetta cheese,
 crumbled
1 egg, lightly beaten
2 sheets ready-rolled
 puff pastry
1 egg, lightly beaten,
 extra

1. Preheat oven to moderately hot 210°C (190°C gas). Brush two oven trays with melted butter or oil. Heat oil in a large heavy-based pan. Add onion and cook over medium heat for 3 minutes, until soft. Transfer to a large mixing bowl. Wash silverbeet leaves and tear into pieces. Place in pan, cover with lid and cook for 30 seconds, until soft. Do this in two batches, shaking pan often and lifting leaves with tongs to prevent them sticking to the base. Set aside to cool.
2. Take handfuls of softened leaves and squeeze lightly to drain out as much moisture as possible. Chop and add to bowl with the cheeses; mix well. Add egg to the mixture, combine thoroughly.
3. Cut each pastry sheet into four squares. Divide mixture between squares, fold over to form triangles. Brush with extra beaten egg and place on prepared trays. Bake 25 minutes, until golden.

> HINT
> When cooking meat on bamboo skewers, soak them in water for 30 minutes before using. This will prevent them from burning.

Beef Satay Skewers with Quick Peanut Sauce (top) and Fetta Triangles.

Spring Rolls

Preparation time:
  25 minutes
Total cooking time:
  10 minutes
Makes 8

1 tablespoon oil
200 g pork mince
2 small carrots, coarsely
  grated
2 spring onions, finely
  chopped
60 g Chinese cabbage,
  finely shredded
60 g bean sprouts,
  roughly chopped
1 small red capsicum, cut
  into short thin strips
2 cloves garlic, crushed
1 teaspoon grated fresh
  ginger
8 large spring roll
  wrappers
oil for deep frying
soy sauce, to serve

1. Heat oil in a heavy-based frying pan; add pork mince. Cook over medium heat for 5 minutes, until mince is browned and almost all the liquid has evaporated. Remove mince with a slotted spoon and set aside to cool slightly.
2. Place vegetables, garlic and ginger in a large mixing bowl; use hands to combine thoroughly. Transfer to frying pan and stir-fry for 2 minutes until soft. Combine vegetables and mince in large bowl; mix well.
3. Working one at a time, place spring roll wrapper diagonally on work surface. Place about half cup of mixture across front half of wrapper, fold the corner closest to you back over filling. Tuck in sides and roll up. Moisten corner with water to secure. Repeat with remaining filling and wrappers.
4. Heat oil in a medium heavy-based pan. Gently lower spring rolls into hot oil. Cook over medium-high heat for 1–2 minutes or until crisp and golden. Cook only one or two at a time. Carefully remove with tongs or slotted spoon. Drain on paper towel; serve spring rolls hot, with soy sauce to dip them into.

> HINT
> You can buy spring roll wrappers at Asian supermarkets. If you don't use the whole packet, the remainder may be frozen. Once defrosted, they should be kept in the refrigerator.

Spring Rolls.

When mince is browned, remove from pan with slotted spoon.

Use your hands to combine thoroughly the vegetables, garlic and ginger.

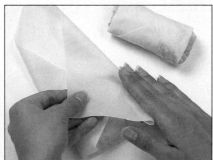

Tuck in end and sides of spring roll wrapper and roll up.

Gently lower spring rolls into hot oil, one or two at a time.

11

Cheesy Corn Muffins

Preparation time:
  10 minutes
Total cooking time:
  20 minutes
Makes 12

3/4 cup self-raising
  flour
1/4 teaspoon salt
1/2 cup cornmeal (fine
  polenta)
3/4 cup grated tasty
  cheese
30 g can corn kernels
2 eggs, lightly beaten
1/3 cup milk
1/4 cup oil

1. Preheat oven to
moderate 180°C.
Brush eight muffin
cups (1/3 cup capacity)
with melted butter
or oil.
2. Sift flour and salt
into a large mixing
bowl. Add cornmeal,
cheese and corn
kernels; make a well in
the centre. Pour
combined eggs, milk
and oil onto the dry
ingredients.
3. Using a wooden
spoon, stir until
ingredients are just
combined. Do not
overbeat. Spoon
mixture into prepared
muffin tins. Bake for
20 minutes, until
puffed and golden.
Remove from tins
immediately and
serve warm.

Mini Corn Dogs

Preparation time:
  10 minutes
Total cooking time:
  1 minute per batch
Makes 16

8 large frankfurts
8 wooden satay sticks
cornflour for dusting
oil for deep-frying
tomato sauce for
  dipping

Batter
2 cups self-raising
  flour
1 egg, lightly beaten
1 tablespoon oil
1 1/2 cups water

1. Cut frankfurts
crossways in half. Cut
satay sticks in half.
Insert a satay stick into
each frankfurt. Dust
the frankfurts with a
little cornflour.
2. *To make Batter:* Sift
flour into a medium
mixing bowl; make a
well in the centre. Add
combined egg, oil and
water gradually. Stir
until all liquid is
incorporated and batter
is free of lumps.
3. Heat oil to
moderately hot in a
deep heavy-based pan.
Holding the satay stick,
dip frankfurts into
batter a few at a time;
allow the excess batter
to drain off. Using
tongs or a slotted
spoon, gently lower
frankfurts into oil.
Cook over medium
high heat for 1 minute
or until golden and
crisp and heated
through. Carefully
remove from oil. Drain
on paper towel, keep
warm. Repeat with
remaining frankfurts.
Serve with tomato
sauce as a dip.

Note: The satay sticks
are left in the frankfurts
during cooking.

> HINT
> For extra flavour,
> add 1 teaspoon of
> chopped fresh chilli
> (you can buy it in
> jars) or a pinch of
> chilli powder to the
> corn dog batter.

Cheesy Corn Muffins (top) and Mini Corn Dogs.

Vegetable Fritters

Preparation time:
  30 minutes
Total cooking time:
  3 minutes each batch
Serves 4–6

1 cup plain flour
1 egg
1 cup water
100 g broccoli
1 small onion
1 small carrot
1 small red capsicum
oil for deep frying

1. Sift flour into a large mixing bowl. Make a well in the centre, add the egg and water and whisk until combined. Cover bowl with plastic wrap and refrigerate for 10 minutes.
2. Cut broccoli into small florets. Finely slice onion, and cut capsicum and carrot into thin strips about 6 cm long. Add vegetables to batter, stir to combine.
3. Heat oil in a medium heavy-based pan. Using tongs, pick up two or three pieces of batter-coated vegetables at a time and lower into oil. Hold submerged in oil a few seconds until batter begins to set and vegetables hold together. Release from tongs and cook until crisp and golden. Drain on paper towel and serve with sweet chilli or soy sauce.

Salmon Fritters

Preparation time:
  20 minutes
Total cooking time:
  6 minutes
Serves 4

415 g can pink salmon
1 medium potato
1 spring onion, finely
  chopped
1 tablespoon
  breadcrumbs
1 egg, lightly beaten
2 tablespoons oil

Quick Tomato Salsa
1 medium tomato,
  finely chopped
1 spring onion, finely
  chopped
1 clove garlic, crushed
2 teaspoons finely
  chopped parsley
1 teaspoon red wine
  vinegar

1. Drain salmon thoroughly and place in a large mixing bowl. Flake with a fork. Grate potato, squeeze out excess liquid; add to salmon. Add spring onion, breadcrumbs and egg to bowl; mix well.
2. Divide mixture into eight portions and shape into patties about 7 cm in diameter. Heat oil in a frying pan and cook fritters over a medium heat for 3 minutes each side, until golden. Serve with tomato salsa.
3. *To make Quick Tomato Salsa:* Place tomato, spring onion, garlic, parsley and wine vinegar in a medium mixing bowl and combine thoroughly.

HINT
To save time, use a purchased bottled tomato salsa instead of making it yourself. Salsa can be found in the Mexican section of supermarkets, in mild, medium and hot varieties.

Vegetable Fritters (top) and Salmon Fritters.

Corn and Potato Fritters

Preparation time:
  15 minutes
Total cooking time:
  4 minutes per batch
Makes about 20

2 large potatoes,
  peeled, grated
260 g can corn kernels,
  drained
4 eggs, lightly beaten
1/2 cup dried
  breadcrumbs
6 spring onions,
  chopped
1 teaspoon garam
  masala
1/4 cup oil

Dipping Sauce
2/3 cup plain yoghurt
2 tablespoons fresh
  chopped mint
2 teaspoons sweet chilli
  sauce

1. Drain grated potato on paper towel, squeeze out excess moisture.
2. Combine potato in a medium bowl with corn, eggs, breadcrumbs, spring onions and garam masala. Mix well.
3. Heat two tablespoons of the oil in a heavy-based frying pan. Drop heaped tablespoons of mixture into pan, cook over medium heat for 2 minutes on each side or until golden brown. Drain on paper towel; keep warm. Repeat with remaining mixture; add extra oil to pan, if necessary.
4. **To make Dipping Sauce:** Combine all ingredients. Mix well. Serve with potato fritters.

Variation: You could use one cup of frozen corn instead of canned.

Crispy Cheese and Curry Lentil Balls

Preparation time:
  15 minutes
Total cooking time:
  1 minute per batch
Makes about 30

1 cup red lentils
4 spring onions,
  chopped
2 cloves garlic, crushed
1 teaspoon ground
  cumin
1 cup fresh
  breadcrumbs
1 cup grated cheddar
  cheese
1 large zucchini, grated
1 cup cornmeal (polenta)
oil for deep frying

1. Place lentils in a medium pan, cover with water. Bring to the boil, reduce heat to low, cover, simmer for 10 minutes until lentils are tender. Drain, rinse under cold water.
2. Combine half the lentils in a food processor bowl or blender with spring onions and garlic. Using the pulse action, press button for five seconds or until mixture is pulpy. Transfer to a large bowl; add remaining lentils, cumin, breadcrumbs, cheese and zucchini, stir until combined.
3. Using hands, roll level tablespoons of mixture into balls, toss lightly in cornmeal.
4. Heat oil in a heavy-based pan. Gently lower small batches of mixture into moderately hot oil. Cook over medium-high heat for 1 minute or until golden brown, crisp and heated through. Carefully remove from oil with tongs or a slotted spoon, drain on paper towel. Repeat with remaining mixture. Serve hot.

Note: These are delicious served with chutney or yoghurt as a dip.

Corn and Potato Fritters (top)
and Crispy Cheese and Curry Lentil Balls.

Fried Calamari with Tartare Sauce

Preparation time:
  20 minutes
Total cooking time:
  1 minute per batch
Serves 4

500 g (about 8) small,
  cleaned calamari
  tubes
2 tablespoons cornflour
2 eggs, lightly beaten
2 cloves garlic, crushed
2 teaspoons grated
  lemon rind
1 cup dried
  breadcrumbs
oil for deep frying

Tartare Sauce
1 cup mayonnaise
2 tablespoons chopped
  chives
2 tablespoons chopped
  pickled onions
1 tablespoon seeded
  mustard

1. Slice calamari thinly.
Toss calamari in
cornflour; shake off
excess. Dip into
combined egg, garlic
and lemon rind. Coat
with breadcrumbs;
shake off excess.
2. Heat oil in a deep
heavy-based pan.
Gently lower small
batches of calamari
into moderately hot oil.
Cook over medium-
high heat for 1 minute
or until just heated
through and lightly
browned. Carefully
remove from oil with a
slotted spoon. Drain on
paper towel, keep
warm. Repeat with
remaining calamari.
3. **To make Tartare
Sauce:** Combine
mayonnaise, chives,
pickled onions and
mustard. Mix well.
Serve as a dip.

Vegetable Vol-au-vents with Creamy Pesto

Preparation time:
  15 minutes
Total cooking time:
  8 minutes
Serves 4

Creamy Pesto
1/2 cup firmly packed
  fresh basil leaves
1/4 cup cream
2 tablespoons grated
  parmesan cheese
1–2 tablespoons oil
1 clove garlic, crushed

Vegetable Filling
2 tablespoons oil
1 small onion, cut in
  wedges
125 g cherry tomatoes,
  halved
125 g button
  mushrooms, sliced
1/2 avocado, peeled and
  chopped
1 tablespoon balsamic
  vinegar

4 x 100 mm purchased
  vol-au-vent cases

1. Preheat oven to
moderate 180°C.
**To make Creamy
Pesto:** Combine basil,
cream, cheese, oil and
garlic in a food
processor or blender.
Process for 20 seconds
or until mixture is
smooth and creamy.
Transfer to small bowl,
cover with plastic wrap.
2. **To make Vegetable
Filling:** Heat oil in a
medium pan, add
onion. Stir-fry over
medium heat for
1 minute or until soft.
Add cherry tomatoes
and mushrooms, stir-
fry for 1 minute or
until just tender. Add
chopped avocado and
vinegar; remove pan
from heat.
3. Place vol-au-vent
cases on an oven tray
and bake for 5 minutes
or until heated
through. Spoon some
warm vegetable filling
into each case and top
with a little pesto.
Serve immediately.

*Fried Calamari with Tartare Sauce (top)
and Vegetable Vol-au-vents with Creamy Pesto.*

Lamb Kebabs with Mango Relish

Preparation time:
15 minutes
Total cooking time:
10–15 minutes
Serves 4

500 g boneless lamb
4 spring onions
1/3 cup hoisin sauce

Mango Relish
1 tablespoon oil
1 onion, chopped
2 small red chillies,
  chopped
1 large mango, peeled,
  chopped
2 tablespoons white
  wine vinegar
2 tablespoons sugar

1. Trim lamb of excess fat and sinew. Cut lamb into 3 cm cubes. Cut spring onions into 3 cm lengths. Thread lamb and spring onions alternately onto bamboo skewers. (Soak skewers for 15 minutes before using.)
2. Place kebabs onto a cold, lightly oiled grill tray. Brush with hoisin sauce. Cook kebabs under high heat for 4 minutes on each side or until cooked as desired, brushing occasionally with hoisin sauce.
3. *To make Mango Relish:* Heat oil in a medium pan, add onion and chillies, stir over medium heat for 2 minutes or until onion is tender. Add mango, vinegar and sugar, bring to the boil. Reduce heat to low, simmer, uncovered, for 5 minutes or until mixture has a pulpy consistency. Serve with lamb kebabs.

Note: Use a bottled chutney or relish as a shortcut.

HINT
For this recipe, you could use lamb fillets (they are not inexpensive, but there is almost no waste), or another lean cut of lamb. Another option is to ask your butcher to bone out a leg of lamb, and cut it into cubes. Do not overcook the lamb. Traditionally served well done, it is becoming most acceptable to serve it slightly pink and the result is moister and more tender.

Lamb Kebabs with Mango Relish.

Chilli Burgers

Preparation time:
  15 minutes
Total cooking time:
  10 minutes
Makes 4

1/2 *cup canned red*
  kidney beans
250 g *sausage mince*
2 *tablespoons tomato*
  paste
1 *onion, finely*
  chopped
1 1/2 *teaspoons chilli*
  sauce
1 *teaspoon ground*
  cumin
4 *hamburger buns*

Filling
1 *avocado, chopped*
1 *small green capsicum,*
  chopped
1 *medium ripe tomato,*
  chopped
1/2 *cup grated cheddar*
  cheese
1/3 *cup sour cream*

1. Place beans in a
medium bowl, mash
slightly with a fork.
Add mince, tomato
paste, onion, chilli
sauce and cumin, stir
until combined. Divide
mixture into four, press
into flat patties.
2. Place patties on a
cold, lightly oiled grill
tray, cook under high
heat for 3 minutes on
each side or until

golden brown and
cooked through.
3. ***To make Filling:***
In a small bowl,
combine avocado,
capsicum, tomato,
cheese and sour cream.
4. Split hamburger
buns in half, toast
lightly under hot grill.
Top buns with patties
and filling.

Note: Adjust the
amount of chilli sauce
to suit your taste.

Burgers with the Works

Preparation time:
  20 minutes
Total cooking time:
  16 minutes
Serves 4

650 g *beef mince*
1 *medium onion, finely*
  chopped
1 *tablespoon*
  worcestershire sauce
2 *tablespoons tomato*
  sauce
1/2 *cup breadcrumbs*
1 *egg, lightly beaten*
2 *teaspoons oil*
4 *slices cheddar cheese*
4 *round bread rolls*
4 *lettuce leaves*
1 *medium tomato, sliced*
4 *slices beetroot*
tomato or barbecue
  sauce

1. Place mince, onion,
sauces, breadcrumbs
and egg in a large
mixing bowl. Using
hands, combine mixture
thoroughly. Divide into
four equal portions and
shape into patties about
1.5 cm thick.
2. Heat frying pan and
brush lightly with oil.
Cook burgers over
medium-high heat for
8 minutes each side,
turning once. Place a
slice of cheese on top
of each burger for the
last 4 minutes of
cooking time.
3. While burgers are
cooking, cut rolls in
half horizontally and
toast lightly under the
griller. Place lettuce,
tomato and beetroot on
each roll, top with
burger. Add tomato or
barbecue sauce to taste,
place top half of roll on
top. Serve immediately.

Note: Try sliced
pineapple, grilled bacon
or fried egg on burgers.

HINT
Make up a double
quantity of burger
mixture and freeze
one batch for future
use. Form into
patties, separate with
plastic wrap and
place in plastic bag.

Chilli Burgers (top) and Burgers with the Works.

Lamb Burger with Cheese and Bacon

Preparation time:
  15 minutes
Total cooking time:
  6 minutes
Makes 4

400 g minced lamb
1 onion, finely chopped
2 teaspoons fresh
  chopped rosemary
1/4 cup tomato paste
4 rashers bacon, rind
  removed
4 slices tasty cheese
4 hamburger buns
2 tablespoons French
  mustard
1 medium carrot, finely
  grated
1 cup finely shredded
  lettuce

1. Combine lamb, onion, rosemary and tomato paste in a medium bowl. Divide mixture into four, shape into flat burgers.
2. Wrap a bacon rasher around each burger, secure with a toothpick.
3. Place on a cold, lightly oiled grill tray, cook under high heat for 3 minutes on each side or until cooked through. Place a slice of cheese on each burger,
remove from heat. Remove toothpick.
4. Split hamburger buns in half, grill on each side until lightly toasted. Spread base of buns with mustard, top with burgers, carrot and lettuce. Place top of roll on top. Serve.

Chick Pea and Ricotta Burgers

Preparation time:
  15 minutes
Total cooking time:
  4 minutes
Makes 4

400 g can chick peas,
  drained
4 spring onions,
  chopped
1/3 cup chopped fresh
  parsley
2 cloves garlic, crushed
plain flour
1 egg, lightly beaten
1/2 cup dry
  breadcrumbs
oil for shallow frying
4 wholemeal bread rolls
2 tablespoons whole
  egg mayonnaise
1 cup alfalfa sprouts

Ricotta Filling
125 g ricotta cheese
1 stick celery, chopped
1 tablespoon seeded
  mustard
2 tablespoons fresh
  chopped chives

1. Combine chick peas, spring onions, parsley and garlic in food processor bowl or blender. Process for 10 seconds or until ingredients are just combined. Press ingredients together in the hands. Divide mixture into four, press into flat patties.
2. Dust patties with flour; shake off excess. Dip patties into egg, coat with breadcrumbs.
3. Heat oil in a heavy-based pan; add patties. Cook over medium heat 2 minutes on each side or until golden brown. Remove, drain on paper towel.
4. **To make Ricotta Filling:** Combine ricotta, celery, mustard and chives. Mix well. Split bread rolls in half, spread with mayonnaise. Top rolls with patties, ricotta filling and alfalfa sprouts. Serve.

HINT
Grow your own alfalfa sprouts from seed – it only takes two to three days.

Lamb Burger with Cheese and Bacon (top) and Chick Pea and Ricotta Burgers.

Muffins with Ham, Cheese and Pineapple

Preparation time:
  15 minutes
Total cooking time:
  10 minutes
Makes 4

4 English muffins
2 tablespoons seeded
  mustard
1 tablespoon oil
1 leek, sliced
4 round ham steaks
4 pineapple rings,
  drained
4 eggs
4 slices cheddar cheese

1. Split muffins in half, toast on each side; spread with mustard.
2. Heat oil in a pan, add leek, stir-fry over medium heat 1 minute or until soft. Remove from pan, place on four muffin halves.
3. Add ham steaks to pan, cook for 1 minute on each side or until lightly browned. Remove from pan, place on top of leek. Repeat with pineapple.
4. Break eggs one at a time into a cup, slide into pan. Cook over low heat for 1 minute or until cooked as desired. Remove from pan, place on top of pineapple. Place cheese on top of eggs, place on grill tray, cook under medium heat for 1 minute or until just melted. Top with remaining muffin halves. Serve.

Variation: You could use bread rolls instead of muffins.

Sesame Pork Burgers

Preparation time:
  15 minutes
Total cooking time:
  10 minutes
Makes 4

400 g pork and veal
  mince
1/3 cup rolled oats
1 tablespoon sesame
  seeds
2 teaspoons soy sauce
2 cloves garlic, crushed
1 teaspoon grated fresh
  ginger
1/3 cup plum sauce
4 bread rolls

Filling
1 tablespoon sesame oil
1/2 red capsicum,
  chopped
2 spring onions,
  chopped
2 cups chopped bok choy

1. Combine mince in a medium bowl with oats, sesame seeds, soy sauce, garlic and ginger. Divide into four equal portions, shape into flat patties.
2. Place onto a cold, lightly oiled grill tray, brush with a little plum sauce, cook under high heat for 4 minutes on each side or until cooked through. Brush burgers with plum sauce occasionally during cooking.
3. *To make Filling:* Heat sesame oil in a frying pan, add capsicum and spring onions, stir-fry over medium heat for 2 minutes or until tender. Add bok choy, stir until combined, remove from heat.
4. Split bread rolls in half, toast lightly. Top with burgers and filling. Serve.

> HINT
> Sesame oil, found in Asian shops and some supermarkets, has a strong, distinctive taste. If you don't like it, peanut oil will give a good nutty flavour.

Ham, Cheese and Pineapple Muffins (top) and Sesame Pork Burgers.

Hot Chicken Fillet Rolls

Preparation time:
  20 minutes
Total cooking time:
  8 minutes
Serves 4

4 chicken breast fillets
1/2 cup cornflour
2 eggs, lightly beaten
1 cup breadcrumbs
2 tablespoons Cajun
  chicken seasoning
2 tablespoons oil
4 round bread rolls
4 lettuce leaves
1/2 cup creamy ranch
  dressing or mayonnaise

1. Trim chicken of excess fat and sinew. Flatten each fillet out slightly with rolling pin. Toss chicken in flour, shake off excess. Dip into egg a piece at a time, then coat with combined breadcrumbs and seasoning.
2. Heat oil in heavy-based frying pan; add chicken. Cook over medium heat 4 minutes each side, turning once. Drain on paper towel.
3. Cut rolls in half horizontally, place a lettuce leaf on each roll. Top with chicken fillet and dollop of dressing.

Hot Chicken Fillet Rolls (top) and Herbed Chicken Rissoles.

Herbed Chicken Rissoles

Preparation:
  10 minutes
Total cooking time:
  12 minutes
Serves 4

500 g chicken mince
1 cup (about 60 g)
  fresh white
  breadcrumbs
1 large onion, finely
  chopped
2 tablespoons chopped
  fresh chives
2 tablespoons chopped
  fresh parsley
1 tablespoon fresh
  thyme leaves
2 teaspoons
  worcestershire sauce
1 egg, lightly beaten
90 g fetta cheese,
  crumbled
freshly ground black
  pepper to taste
1/2 cup fruit chutney

1. Place chicken mince in a bowl. Add breadcrumbs, onion, chives, parsley, thyme, worcestershire sauce and egg and stir until combined.
2. Divide the mixture into eight equal portions and shape into rissoles about 1.5 cm thick.
3. Place rissoles on a cold, lightly oiled grill tray and cook under high heat for 5 minutes on each side or until browned and cooked through.
4. Top each rissole with fetta cheese and sprinkle with pepper. Cook until cheese has melted. Top with a spoonful of chutney. Rissoles may be served in bread rolls, if desired.

Note: For convenience, you can mix up the rissoles a day ahead. Keep them, covered, in the refrigerator until ready to cook.

> HINT
> To make a more elaborate meal, serve fetta as a side dish with the rissoles. Combine the fetta with 1 tablespoon of chopped mint, 2 tablespoons of olive oil and 1 tablespoon of lemon juice.

Beef Tacos

Preparation time:
  20 minutes
Total cooking time:
  10 minutes
Serves 4

1 tablespoon oil
1 small onion, finely
  chopped
500 g beef mince
35 g packet taco
  seasoning mix
1/4 cup water
1/2 cup taco sauce
8 taco shells
4 lettuce leaves, finely
  shredded
1 large tomato,
  chopped
1 cup grated cheddar
  cheese

1. Heat oil in frying pan. Cook onion over medium heat for 3 minutes, until soft. Add mince; cook for 3 minutes until browned. Use a fork to break up any lumps of mince as it cooks.
2. Add seasoning mix, water and taco sauce to mince and stir over medium heat for 3 minutes, or until thickened.
3. To serve, place some of the mince mixture in the base of each taco shell. Top with lettuce, tomato and grated cheese.

Beef and Bean Burritos

Preparation time:
  30 minutes
Total cooking time:
  30 minutes
Serves 4

2 tablespoons oil
1 medium onion,
  sliced
1 tablespoon ground
  cumin
2 teaspoons ground
  coriander
1/2 teaspoon ground
  cinnamon
1 teaspoon chilli
  powder
600 g minced beef
425 g can tomatoes,
  chopped
1/3 cup tomato paste
440 g can kidney
  beans, drained
270 g can corn kernels
1 packet flour tortillas

Topping
160 g cheddar cheese,
  grated
1/4 cup taco sauce,
  optional

1. Heat oil in a large heavy-based pan; add onion, spices and mince. Cook over medium-high heat for 10 minutes until well browned and almost all the liquid has evaporated. Use a fork to break up any lumps of mince as it cooks. Reduce heat to low, add tomatoes and paste. Cover and cook, stirring occasionally, for 20 minutes. Add kidney beans and corn and stir until heated through.
2. Preheat oven to 180°C. To assemble burritos, place about half a cup of mince mixture on each tortilla. Roll tortillas around filling and place seam-side down on baking tray. (Allow two burritos per person.) Sprinkle burritos with grated cheese and bake for 10 minutes or until the cheese has melted. Top each burrito with a tablespoon of taco sauce, if liked, and serve immediately, with a green salad.

Note: Flour tortillas are available in some supermarkets. If you can't find them, you could use pitta bread split in half.

Beef Tacos (top) and Beef and Bean Burritos.

Nachos with Guacamole

Preparation time:
 20 minutes
Total cooking time:
 3–5 minutes
Serves 4

440 g can red kidney
 beans, rinsed,
 drained
1/3 cup bottled tomato
 salsa
250 g packet corn chips
2 cups grated cheddar
 cheese
1 1/2 cups bottled
 tomato salsa, extra
1/3 cup sour cream

Guacamole
1 large avocado
1 spring onion, finely
 chopped
1 small tomato, finely
 chopped
1 tablespoon lemon
 juice
freshly ground black
 pepper to taste

1. Preheat oven to
moderate 180°C.
Combine kidney beans
and salsa, divide the
mixture between four
ovenproof serving
plates. Cover with
corn chips and grated
cheese. Place in oven
and cook for 3–5

minutes, until cheese
has melted.
2. To assemble nachos,
spoon extra salsa onto
melted cheese, top with
guacamole and sour
cream.
3. *To make
Guacamole:* Peel
avocado and remove
stone. Mash flesh
lightly with a fork, and
combine with spring
onion, tomato, lemon
juice and pepper.

Lamb Mini Meatballs with Hot Red Sauce

Preparation time:
 25 minutes
Total cooking time:
 15 minutes
Makes about 10

850 g minced lamb
1 small onion, finely
 chopped
1/4 cup finely chopped
 parsley
1 tablespoon French
 mustard

Hot Red Sauce
2 large red capsicum
1 tablespoon tarragon
 vinegar
2 tablespoons pine
 nuts
2 cloves garlic, crushed
1/4 teaspoon finely
 chopped fresh chilli
1/4 cup olive oil

1. Place mince, onion,
parsley and mustard in
a large mixing bowl
and combine
thoroughly. Roll level
tablespoonfuls of
mixture into 40 balls.
Refrigerate until
required. Thread four
meatballs onto each of
10 skewers.
2. *To make Hot Red
Sauce:* Cut capsicum in
half and remove seeds.
Place skin-side up under
griller and grill until
skin is black. Wrap in a
damp tea-towel until
cool. Rub off skin.
Place capsicum, vinegar,
pine nuts, garlic and
chilli in a food
processor or blender.
Process at medium
speed, adding oil slowly
until smooth. Pour into
serving bowl.
3. Heat grill or frying
pan and brush lightly
with oil. Cook meatball
skewers over medium-
high heat for about
12 minutes until well
browned. Drain on
paper towel and serve
with hot red sauce.

*Nachos with Guacamole (top)
and Lamb Mini Meatballs with Hot Red Sauce.*

Chilli Sausage Dogs

Preparation time:
  20 minutes
Total cooking time:
  10 minutes
Makes 4

1 *medium tomato,*
  finely chopped
1 *small red onion,*
  finely chopped
2 *teaspoons sweet chilli*
  sauce
1 *tablespoon finely*
  chopped basil
2 *teaspoons oil*
4 *herb-and-garlic-*
  flavoured sausages
4 *long bread rolls*

1. Place tomato, onion, chilli sauce and basil in a small bowl; mix well.
2. Heat oil in a frying pan. Prick the sausages all over with a fork, cook over medium heat for 10 minutes, until they are brown and cooked through.
3. Cut a deep slit along top of each roll. Place a sausage in the opening, top with some of the tomato/chilli mixture. Serve immediately.

Note: You can substitute any of your favourite sausages.

Glazed Apricot Ribs

Preparation time:
  5 minutes
Total cooking time:
  30 minutes
Serves 4

1.5 *kg beef spareribs*
1/2 *cup apricot nectar*
1 *tablespoon soy sauce*
1 *tablespoon sweet*
  chilli sauce
2 *cloves garlic, crushed*
2 *teaspoons grated*
  fresh ginger

1. Preheat oven to moderately hot 210°C (190°C gas). Place the spareribs in a single layer in a baking dish.
2. Combine apricot nectar, soy sauce, chilli sauce, garlic and ginger and pour over the spareribs.
3. Bake for 30 minutes or until ribs are tender and well-browned, brushing occasionally with glaze during cooking. Serve.

HINT
The spareribs will have more flavour if you have time to marinate them in the glaze for several hours.

Chilli Sausage Dogs (top)
and Glazed Apricot Ribs.

Chicken Sausage Dogs

Preparation time:
30 minutes
Total cooking time:
5 minutes
Serves 4

Chicken Sausages
400 g chicken mince
3/4 cup fresh
breadcrumbs
1/4 cup fruit chutney
3 cloves garlic, crushed

4 large Lebanese breads
1/2 cup soft cream
cheese
1/2 cup chopped chives

Filling
1 small apple, finely
chopped
1 medium tomato,
finely chopped
1/2 red onion, finely
chopped
2 tablespoons lemon
juice

1. *To make Chicken Sausages:* Combine mince, breadcrumbs, fruit chutney and garlic; divide into eight equal portions. Roll each portion into a sausage shape about 12 cm long. Place onto a cold, oiled grill tray, cook under high heat for 5 minutes or until cooked through; turn sausages occasionally. Drain on paper towel. Keep warm.
2. Split Lebanese breads in half horizontally to give eight rounds. Combine cream cheese and chives; spread over bread halves.
3. *To make Filling:* Combine apple, tomato, onion and lemon juice. Spoon onto one side of bread halves.
4. Place sausages onto bread halves with filling. Roll bread to enclose filling; secure with toothpicks. Serve.

Club Sandwich

Preparation time:
15 minutes
Total cooking time:
Nil
Serves 4

12 slices bread

Tuna Filling
185 g can tuna, drained
1 tablespoon mayonnaise
1 teaspoon curry
powder
8 gherkins, sliced
lengthways

Salad
1/2 iceberg lettuce
1 large tomato, sliced
1 Lebanese cucumber,
sliced

1. In a small bowl, combine the tuna, mayonnaise and curry powder.
2. Spread four slices of bread with tuna filling and top with gherkin slices. Top each with a slice of bread.
3. Arrange lettuce, tomato and cucumber in layers and top with remaining bread.
4. Cut sandwiches diagonally in half; insert a toothpick in each to hold the layers in place.

Variation: The bread may be toasted, if you prefer. Other fillings may be used: curried egg, sliced roast beef and chutney or chicken and avocado or bacon.

HINT
Sandwiches are best made just before serving. If you have to make them ahead, cover with a clean damp tea-towel and refrigerate.

Chicken Sausage Dogs (top) and Club Sandwich.

Cut pastry into rounds and press into large muffin tins.

For filling, cook mince until well browned. Use a fork to break up lumps.

Meat Pies

Preparation time:
  20 minutes
Total cooking time:
  25 minutes
Makes 16

4 sheets ready rolled
  shortcrust pastry
2 small tomatoes, sliced
1/2 teaspoon dried
  oregano leaves

Filling
1 tablespoon oil
1 onion, chopped
2 cloves garlic,
  crushed
500 g minced beef
2 tablespoons plain
  flour
1 1/2 cups beef stock
1/3 cup tomato sauce
2 teaspoons
  worcestershire sauce
1 tablespoon chopped
  fresh rosemary

Meat Pies.

1. Preheat oven to moderately hot 210°C (190°C gas). Cut pastry into circles using a round, 10 cm fluted cutter. Press pastry circles into large muffin tins (1/3-cup capacity).
2. *To make Filling:* Heat oil in a heavy-based pan; add onion and garlic. Cook over medium heat for 2 minutes or until onion is soft. Add mince, cook over high heat for 3 minutes or until well browned and all the liquid has evaporated. Use a fork to break up any lumps of mince as it cooks.
3. Add flour, stir until combined, cook over medium heat for 1 minute. Add stock, sauces and rosemary, stir over heat until boiling. Reduce heat to low, simmer for 5 minutes or until mixture has reduced and thickened; stir occasionally. Remove pan from heat, allow to cool.
4. Divide filling between pastry circles. Top each with a slice of tomato, sprinkle with oregano. Bake for 25 minutes or until pastry is golden brown and crisp. Serve hot.

HINT
To make traditional meat pies, follow the recipe up to the last step and cut out rounds of puff pastry to fit the top. Place the pastry rounds over the tomato and oregano topping, seal the edges with beaten egg. Bake until the pastry is puffed and golden.

Cook filling mixture until it has reduced and thickened, stirring occasionally.

Fill pastry cases and top each with a slice of tomato and sprinkling of oregano.

39

San Choy Bow

Preparation time:
  10 minutes
Total cooking time:
  10 minutes
Serves 4

1 tablespoon oil
1 onion, chopped
1 small red capsicum,
  chopped
1 clove garlic, crushed
1 teaspoon sambal
  oelek
200 g pork and veal
  mince
1 cup coconut milk
2 tablespoons peanut
  butter
1 tablespoon lemon
  juice
2 teaspoons soy sauce
8 lettuce cups

1. Heat oil in a large frying pan, add onion, capsicum, garlic and sambal oelek, stir-fry over medium heat for 2 minutes or until onion is soft.
2. Add mince, stir-fry over high heat for 3 minutes or until well browned and almost all the liquid has evaporated. Use a fork to break up any lumps of mince as it cooks.
3. Add coconut milk, peanut butter, lemon juice and soy sauce, bring to the boil. Reduce heat to low, simmer, uncovered, for 5 minutes or until almost all the liquid has evaporated. Remove from heat, cool.
4. Spoon mixture into lettuce cups to serve.

Variation: You can use chicken or beef mince if more convenient.

Tandoori Chicken Pockets

Preparation time:
  15 minutes
Total cooking time:
  7 minutes
Serves 4

1/3 cup plain yoghurt
2 tablespoons tandoori
  paste
4 (440 g) chicken thigh
  fillets
4 pitta bread pockets

Filling
1 Lebanese cucumber,
  chopped
1 medium tomato,
  peeled, seeded, chopped
2 tablespoons plain
  yoghurt, extra
2 tablespoons
  desiccated coconut
2 tablespoons chopped
  fresh mint

1. Combine yoghurt and tandoori paste in a medium bowl. Add chicken, stir until chicken is well coated.
2. Place chicken on a cold, lightly oiled grill tray, cook under high heat for 3 minutes on each side or until cooked through. Cool chicken, slice thinly.
3. Grill pitta pockets under high heat for 1 minute or until heated through.
4. *To make Filling:* Combine cucumber, tomato, extra yoghurt, coconut and mint in a medium bowl.
5. Cut pitta pockets crossways in half, fill cavities with chicken and filling. Serve immediately.

> HINT
> To enhance their flavour, you can marinate the chicken fillets in the yoghurt mixture for several hours or even overnight, in the refrigerator.

San Choy Bow (top)
and Tandoori Chicken Pockets.

Salmon Pitta Pockets

Preparation time:
  10 minutes
Total cooking time:
  Nil
Makes 4

Mayonnaise
1 egg yolk
1/2 teaspoon prepared
  mustard
1 tablespoon lime juice
2/3 cup olive oil
salt and white pepper
  to taste

415 g can pink salmon,
  drained
80 g mixed salad leaves
1 medium tomato,
  sliced
4 pitta bread pockets

1. Place egg yolk in a small mixing bowl, add mustard and half the lime juice. Whisk ingredients together for 1 minute until light and creamy. Add oil about a teaspoon at a time, whisking constantly until mixture is thick and creamy.
2. Increase addition of oil as the mayonnaise thickens. Continue whisking until all the oil is added. Stir in remaining juice, and salt and pepper to taste.
3. Flake salmon with a fork. Place salad leaves and tomato into pocket breads, top with salmon and mayonnaise. Serve immediately.

Lamb Steak and Onion Sandwich

Preparation time:
  5 minutes
Total cooking time:
  10 minutes
Serves 4

2 tablespoons oil
2 large onions, sliced in
  rings
4 eggs
4 (400 g) lamb
  schnitzels
1 tablespoon
  worcestershire sauce
8 slices bread
2 tablespoons tomato
  sauce
2 medium ripe
  tomatoes, sliced
215 g can sliced
  beetroot, well drained

1. Heat oil in a large frying pan, add onions, stir over medium heat for 3 minutes or until tender and brown, remove from pan.
2. Break the eggs into a cup, one at a time, and slide into the frying pan. Cook for 1 minute or more if desired, remove from the pan. Keep warm.
3. Add schnitzels to pan, cook for 1–2 minutes on each side. Add worcestershire sauce, allow to coat the schnitzels, remove from pan.
4. Toast bread slices on each side. Spread four slices with tomato sauce, top with the onions, eggs, lamb, tomato and beetroot. Place remaining toast on top. Slice diagonally. Serve.

Note: Lamb schnitzels are thin lean lamb steaks. If your butcher doesn't stock schnitzels you could substitute lamb fillets. Slice each one lengthways without cutting right through it so you can open it out, and pound slightly to flatten.
To make a traditional steak sandwich, use slices of beef eye fillet or very thin slices of rump steak instead of the lamb.

*Salmon Pitta Pockets (top) and
Lamb Steak and Onion Sandwich.*

Potato Wedges with Herb Dip

Preparation time:
  15 minutes
Total cooking time:
  4 minutes
Serves 4

1 kg potatoes
oil for deep frying

Creamy Herb Dip
1/2 cup sour cream
2 tablespoons plain
  yoghurt
2 tablespoons chopped
  chives
1 tablespoon chopped
  fresh thyme
1 clove garlic, crushed
1 teaspoon sweet chilli
  sauce

1. Peel potatoes, cut
each into about
10 wedges. Dry wedges
with paper towel.
2. Heat oil in a deep
heavy-based pan. Gently
lower potato wedges
into moderately hot oil.
Cook over medium-
high heat for 4 minutes
or until golden brown.
Remove from oil, drain
on paper towel.
3. *To make Creamy
Herb Dip:* Combine
sour cream and
yoghurt. Mix in chives,
thyme, garlic and chilli
sauce. Serve as dip with
hot potato wedges.

Chips

Preparation time:
  20 minutes
Total cooking time:
  6 minutes
Serves 4

1.2 kg old potatoes
oil for deep frying
chicken salt, to taste

1. Peel potatoes, rinse
and pat dry with paper
towels. Cut lengthways
into slices 7 mm thick.
Then cut each piece
into 7 mm-wide chips.
2. Heat oil in a deep,
heavy-based pan.
Gently lower potatoes,
a few chips at a time,
into the moderately hot
oil. Cook over a
medium-high heat for
3 minutes, until pale
golden. Carefully
remove with tongs.
Drain on paper towel,
repeat with remaining
chips. Allow to cool.
3. When ready to serve,
reheat oil. Cook chips
again, in batches, until
crisp and golden. Drain
on paper towel,
sprinkle with chicken
salt. Serve immediately.

Note: The secret of
really crisp chips is in
the double cooking.

French Loaf Grill

Preparation time:
  10 minutes
Total cooking time:
  3 minutes
Makes 8

80 g butter, softened
1 clove garlic, crushed
1 tablespoon
  wholegrain mustard
2 teaspoons lemon
  juice
1 long French bread
  stick
385 g can asparagus
  spears
4 slices leg ham
80 g gruyère cheese,
  sliced

1. Place butter, garlic,
mustard and lemon
juice in a small bowl;
mix well. Cut French
stick into four equal
sections, then in halves
horizontally. Spread
both cut sides with the
butter mixture.
2. Drain asparagus
spears thoroughly. Lay
on buttered side of
bread, top with half
slice ham and cheese.
3. Place under
moderately hot grill
and cook for about
3 minutes, until cheese
has melted. Serve.

---

*From top: Chips, French Loaf Grill and
Potato Wedges with Herb Dip.*

Chicken Filo Parcels

Preparation time:
  20 minutes
Total cooking time:
  20 minutes
Makes 6

1 barbecued chicken
12 sheets filo pastry
1/4 cup oil
1 large avocado, sliced
2 small tomatoes, sliced
1 cup grated cheddar
  cheese
3 spring onions, finely
  sliced
30 g butter, melted

1. Preheat oven to moderately hot 210°C (190°C gas). Brush baking tray with oil. Remove meat from barbecued chicken, including skin. Shred meat, discard carcass.
2. Lay one sheet of filo on work surface, short edge to front, brush lightly with oil. Top with second sheet. Place one sixth of chicken in oblong pile about 10 cm in from end and 5 cm in from sides. Lay slices of avocado and tomato on top, sprinkle with cheese and onions.
3. Fold end of pastry over filling, tuck in sides and roll up to form a parcel. Brush with butter. Repeat with remaining ingredients. Bake 20 minutes. Serve.

Pork Sausages in Pitta

Preparation time:
  15 minutes
Total cooking time:
  8 minutes
Serves 4

500 g pork mince
1/4 cup grated apple
2 spring onions, finely
  chopped
2 cabbage leaves, finely
  shredded
4 pitta pocket breads
1/3 cup plum sauce

1. Place mince, apple and onion in bowl. Using hands, combine thoroughly. Divide mixture into four portions and form into sausage shapes.
2. Heat frying pan and brush with oil. Cook sausages over medium heat for 8 minutes, turning occasionally, until well browned.
3. Divide cabbage between pocket breads, place sausages on top and drizzle with plum sauce. Serve immediately.

Chicken Filo Parcels (left) and Pork Sausages in Pitta.

Spicy Chicken Pasties

Preparation time:
  20 minutes
Total cooking time:
  30 minutes
Makes 8

1 tablespoon oil
1 small onion, finely
  chopped
1 clove garlic, crushed
1 teaspoon curry
  powder
150 g chicken mince
2 tablespoons frozen
  peas
2 teaspoons finely
  chopped fresh
  coriander
2 sheets ready-rolled
  puff pastry
1 egg, lightly beaten

1. Preheat oven to moderate 180°C. Heat oil in a heavy-based frying pan. Add onion, cook over medium heat 2 minutes, or until onion is soft. Add garlic and curry powder, cook, stirring, a further 1 minute.
2. Add chicken to pan, cook for 8 minutes or until mince is cooked through and almost all the liquid has evaporated. Use a fork to break up any lumps of mince as it cooks. Stir in peas and coriander, transfer to a bowl to cool.
3. Using a plate as a guide, cut 12 cm circles from pastry. Divide chicken mixture between each circle, fold over and pleat edges to seal. Place on a baking tray and brush with beaten egg. Bake for 20 minutes, until golden.

Ham and Cheese Croissants with Mustard Cream

Preparation time:
  10 minutes
Total cooking time:
  5 minutes
Serves 4

4 purchased croissants
4 slices Swiss cheese
4 slices leg ham

Mustard Cream
1/3 cup whole egg
  mayonnaise
1 tablespoon sour cream
1 teaspoon wholegrain
  mustard

1. Preheat oven to moderate 180°C. Slice croissants in half horizontally. Lay a slice of Swiss cheese on each base, place on an oven tray. Place croissant tops, cut-side down on oven tray. Cook for 5 minutes, until cheese has melted and croissants are crisp.
2. Place ham on top of cheese, spread mustard cream on ham and replace top of croissant, serve immediately.
3. *To make Mustard Cream:* Place the mayonnaise, sour cream and mustard in a small bowl and mix well.

Note: You can buy croissants fresh from the bakery, or from the supermarket in packets of four. They freeze very successfully.

> HINT
> Croissants are specially suitable for brunch entertaining. Other filling ideas are: camembert and avocado; chicken with thinly sliced mushrooms and sour cream; smoked salmon with sour cream and capers.

*Spicy Chicken Pasties (top) and
Ham and Cheese Croissants with Mustard Cream.*

Fried Chicken

Preparation time:
  20 minutes
Total cooking time:
  10 minutes
Serves 4

8 chicken drumsticks
2 x 50 g packets cheese
  corn chips
1 cup dried breadcrumbs
1/2 cup plain flour
2 eggs, beaten
oil for deep frying
1 cup bottled salsa or
  taco sauce

1. Remove skin from drumsticks. Cook in a large pan of boiling water for 7 minutes, until just cooked and tender. Drain and cool.
2. Place corn chips and breadcrumbs in food processor. Process for 20 seconds or until corn chips are crushed and mixture is combined.
3. Working one at a time, dip drumsticks in flour, then egg. Coat well with chip mixture. Heat oil in a deep, heavy-based pan. Gently lower drumsticks into moderately hot oil. Cook over medium heat for 2 minutes until crisp and golden. Lift out, drain on paper towel. Serve with salsa.

Chicken Salad Roll-ups

Preparation time:
  15 minutes
Total cooking time:
  5 minutes
Serves 4

500 g chicken thigh
  fillets
1 tablespoon olive oil
1 small onion, sliced
4 sheets lavash
  bread
1/3 cup mayonnaise
4 lettuce leaves, finely
  shredded
2 small tomatoes,
  chopped
1/2 small Lebanese
  cucumber, sliced

1. Trim chicken of excess fat and sinew. Cut into thin strips. Heat oil in a frying pan, cook chicken and onion for 5 minutes, until golden and cooked through.
2. Lay out sheets of lavash bread. Divide chicken mixture into four and place in a pile at the end of each piece of bread. Top with mayonnaise, lettuce, tomato and cucumber.
3. Fold end of bread over filling, tuck in sides and roll up. Serve immediately.

Chicken Salad Roll-ups (left) and Fried Chicken.

Chicken Nuggets with Sweet and Sour Sauce

Preparation time:
  20 minutes
Total cooking time:
  12 minutes
Serves 4

2 *chicken breast fillets*
1/2 *cup plain flour*
1 *egg, lightly beaten*
3/4 *cup cornflake*
  crumbs

Sweet and Sour Sauce
1/4 *cup orange juice*
1/4 *cup pineapple juice*
1/4 *cup white vinegar*
2 *tablespoons soft*
  brown sugar
1 *tablespoon sweet*
  chilli sauce
2 *teaspoons cornflour*
1 *tablespoon water*

1. Preheat oven to moderate 180°C. Line an oven tray with foil. Cut chicken into rough 3 cm cubes. Working a few at a time, dip pieces in flour, shake off excess. Dip into egg, coat with cornflake crumbs. If you have time, refrigerate for 30 minutes.
2. Place nuggets on tray, bake for 10-15 minutes until crisp and golden. Serve with sweet and sour sauce.

3. *To make Sweet and Sour Sauce:* Place juices, vinegar, sugar and chilli sauce in a small pan. Stir over medium heat until sugar has dissolved. Combine cornflour and water in a small bowl until smooth; add to pan. Stir over medium heat until mixture boils and thickens. Reduce heat and simmer for 2 minutes. Transfer to a small bowl to cool. Serve warm or at room temperature.

Spanish Omelette

Preparation time:
  20 minutes
Total cooking time:
  25 minutes
Serves 6

1 *kg medium potatoes*
1 *tablespoon olive oil*
1 *large onion, finely*
  chopped
75 *g sliced salami,*
  chopped
4 *eggs, lightly beaten*

1. Cut potatoes into rough 2 cm cubes and cook in a large pan of boiling water until just tender. Drain and cool.
2. Heat oil in a 25 cm non-stick frying pan. Cook onion for 3 minutes over medium-low heat until soft. Add salami and cook for a further 3 minutes, stirring occasionally.
3. Add potatoes to pan, and cook for 5 minutes, stirring to combine. Try to distribute onion and salami through the potato, so that they are not all on the base of pan. Reduce heat to low; preheat grill to medium heat.
4. Pour eggs into pan, moving potato mixture to let eggs flow through. Cook for 3 minutes, until egg has set around edges and base. Remove pan from the stovetop and place under the grill for 2–3 minutes until the top has set. Invert onto a plate and cut into wedges. Cool to room temperature before serving.

Note: For a different flavour, add some chopped capsicum with the onion.

*Chicken Nuggets with Sweet and Sour Sauce (top)
and Spanish Omelette.*

Rub butter into flour until the mixture is fine and crumbly.

Roll dough out to a rectangle, spread with tomato paste.

Ham and Pineapple Pizza Wheels

Preparation time:
  25 minutes
Total cooking time:
  20 minutes
Serves 4

2 cups self-raising flour
40 g butter, chopped
1/2 cup milk
2 tablespoons tomato
  paste
1 small onion, finely
  chopped
2 pineapple slices,
  finely chopped
100 g sliced ham,
  shredded
1/3 cup grated cheddar
  cheese
1 tablespoon finely
  chopped parsley

1. Preheat oven to moderate 180°C. Brush an oven tray with oil.

Sift flour into bowl. Using fingertips, rub butter into flour for 2 minutes or until fine and crumbly. Add almost all the milk, mix to soft dough, adding more milk if necessary. Turn onto lightly floured surface, knead for 30 seconds.
2. Roll out dough on baking paper to a 20 x 30 cm rectangle, about 5 mm thick. Spread tomato paste over dough, leaving 1 cm edge.
3. Combine onion, pineapple, ham, cheese and parsley, mix well. Spread evenly over tomato paste, leaving a 2 cm edge. Using paper as a guide, roll up dough from long side.
4. Using a sharp knife, cut roll into eight slices. Place cut-side down on tray, bake 20 minutes until golden.

Ham and Pineapple Pizza Wheels.

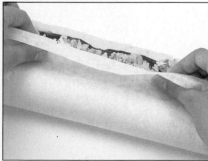

Using paper as a guide, roll up dough from long side.

Cut roll into eight slices and place cut-side down on baking tray.

Fish in Beer Batter with Tartare Sauce

Preparation time:
  15 minutes +
  15 minutes resting
Total cooking time:
  6 minutes
Serves 4

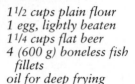

1 1/2 cups plain flour
1 egg, lightly beaten
1 1/4 cups flat beer
4 (600 g) boneless fish
  fillets
oil for deep frying

Tartare Sauce
2/3 cup mayonnaise
1 tablespoon chopped
  capers
1 tablespoon chopped
  gherkins
2 teaspoons finely
  chopped parsley
1 teaspoon lemon juice

1. Sift flour into a large bowl; make a well in the centre. Add egg and beer all at once, whisk until all liquid is incorporated and batter is free of lumps. Leave, covered with plastic wrap, for 15 minutes.
2. Heat oil in large heavy-based pan. Dip fish into batter, then gently lower into moderately hot oil. Cook over medium-high heat for 3–4 minutes, until golden and crisp. Carefully remove from oil with tongs or slotted spoon. Drain on paper towel. Serve immediately with tartare sauce.
3. *To make Tartare Sauce:* Combine mayonnaise, capers, gherkins, parsley and lemon juice in small mixing bowl.

Note: When deep-frying, the pan should only be half full of oil, as the level will rise while cooking. Cook one or two pieces of fish at a time.

Eggplant and Capsicum Grill

Preparation time:
  15 minutes
Total cooking time:
  8 minutes
Serves 4

2 tablespoons oil
1 small eggplant, cut
  into 1 cm slices
1 large focaccia bread
  (30 x 30 cm)
1/3 cup tomato paste
1 small onion, finely
  sliced
1 small red capsicum,
  cut into thin strips
1/4 cup chopped
  coriander leaves
1/2 cup grated cheddar
  cheese
1/4 cup shredded
  parmesan cheese

1. Heat oil in a large frying pan. Cook eggplant slices for 2 minutes, until soft and just golden. Drain on paper towel.
2. Cut bread into four squares, then in half horizontally. Toast each side for 2 minutes, until golden. Spread with tomato paste.
3. Place eggplant, onion, capsicum, coriander and combined cheeses on base of each square. Place under moderately hot grill for 2–3 minutes, until cheese has melted. Serve immediately.

HINT
Almost anything is suitable as foccacia bread topping: try chicken, ham, sliced tomatoes, avocado. Cover your topping with cheese and melt under griller.

Fish in Beer Batter with Tartare Sauce (top) and Eggplant and Capsicum Grill.

The Perfect Jaffle

Preparation time:
  10 minutes
Total cooking time:
  3–5 minutes
Makes 4

8 slices thick toasting
  bread
30 g soft butter
4 slices leg ham
1 large tomato, sliced
1 cup grated cheddar
  cheese
black pepper, to taste

1. Preheat jaffle iron or
toasted sandwich maker.
Spread bread slices
thinly with butter. Place
bread in four stacks of
two, buttered sides
together, to assemble.
2. Place a slice of ham
on each top slice of
bread, top with tomato.
Scatter cheese onto
tomato, spreading out
evenly. Sprinkle with
pepper.
3. Carefully lift top
slice of bread, with
filling, onto sandwich
maker, place other slice
on top, buttered-side
up. Close lid and cook
for 3 minutes, or until
golden. Lift out with
tongs and cut in half.

Note: Toasted sandwiches
can also be made in a

frying pan. Prepare up
to step 3, then lift the
top slice of bread and
filling onto a heated
frying pan. Place the
second piece of bread
on top, buttered-side
up. Cook over a
medium heat for
2–3 minutes, until the
underside is golden.
Using an egg slice,
carefully turn the
sandwich over and
cook the other side.

Savoury Slice

Preparation time:
  25 minutes
Total cooking time:
  30 minutes
Serves 6

2 cups self-raising flour
40 g butter, chopped
3/4 cup grated cheddar
  cheese
1/2 cup milk
1/2 cup chunky tomato
  pasta sauce
1 medium onion, finely
  sliced
100 g sliced salami, cut
  into thin strips
1/2 cup sliced black
  pitted olives
1/4 cup shredded
  parmesan cheese

1. Preheat oven to
moderately hot 210°C
(190°C gas). Brush a
20 x 30 cm shallow
rectangular tin with
melted butter or oil.
Line the base and sides
with baking paper.
2. Place flour, butter
and cheese in food
processor bowl. Using
the pulse action, press
button for 30 seconds
or until mixture is fine
and crumbly. Add
almost all the milk and
process for a further
30 seconds or until
mixture comes together,
adding more liquid if
necessary.
3. Turn mixture onto a
lightly floured surface.
Knead lightly for
2 minutes or until
smooth. Roll out dough
to 20 x 30 cm, and
place in prepared tin.
Spread the dough with
pasta sauce and top
with onion, salami,
olives and parmesan
cheese. Bake for
30 minutes. Lift slice
from the tin and cut
into rectangles to serve.
Serve immediately.

Note: Although this
pizza-like slice is best
eaten hot, leftovers can
be wrapped in plastic,
individually or together,
and frozen. Reheat as
you need them in a
preheated 180°C oven
for 10–15 minutes.

The Perfect Jaffle (top) and Savoury Slice.

Covered Pizzas

Preparation time:
  30 minutes
Total cooking time:
  30 minutes
Serves 4

3 cups plain flour
1 egg, lightly beaten
1/2 cup buttermilk
125 g butter, melted
1 cup bottled tomato
  pasta sauce
100 g sliced salami
100 g button
  mushrooms, sliced
2/3 cup sliced, bottled
  artichokes
1/3 cup fresh basil leaves
3 bocconcini, sliced
1/4 cup grated parmesan
  cheese
milk for glazing
1 1/2 tablespoons
  cornmeal (fine polenta)

1. Preheat oven to moderately hot 210°C (190°C gas). Brush two oven trays lightly with melted butter or oil. Sift flour into a large mixing bowl; add the combined egg, buttermilk and butter. Mix to a soft dough. Turn onto a lightly floured surface, knead for 1 minute or until smooth.
2. Divide the mixture in half and roll each half into a 30 cm round.
3. Divide the pasta sauce, salami, button mushrooms, artichokes, basil, bocconcini and parmesan cheese between the pastry rounds, placing ingredients on one half of each round, leaving a 2 cm border.
4. Brush border of each pastry with milk. Fold pastry over the top to enclose the filling, press the borders together to seal and pinch a frill around the borders. Brush top of pastry with milk, sprinkle with cornmeal. Place on oven trays, bake for 30 minutes or until golden brown.

Note: These covered pizzas (also called calzone) can be assembled an hour ahead; cook them just before serving.

> **HINT**
> Bocconcini are fresh baby mozzarella cheeses, which you will find packaged in the supermarket or loose in the delicatessen. They will keep, covered with water, in the refrigerator for a few days. Change the water daily.

Covered Pizzas.

Add egg, buttermilk and butter to flour; mix to a soft dough.

Divide pastry in half and roll out to two 30 cm rounds.

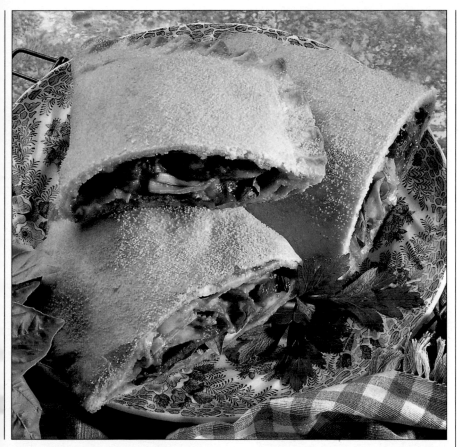

Divide sauce, salami, mushrooms, artichokes, basil and cheeses between pastry.

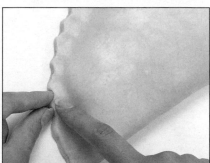

Press edges together to seal and pinch a frill around the borders.

Mini Vegetarian Pizzas

Preparation time:
  20 minutes
Total cooking time:
  20 minutes
Serves 4

1 tablespoon oil
1 small green capsicum,
  cut into short thin
  strips
150 g mushrooms,
  thinly sliced
1 medium zucchini,
  thinly sliced
4 mini pizza bases
2/3 cup purchased
  napolitaine pasta
  sauce
410 g can artichokes,
  drained and quartered
130 g can corn kernels,
  drained
1 cup grated mozzarella
  cheese

1. Preheat oven to moderately hot 210°C (190°C gas). Brush two baking trays lightly with melted butter or oil. Heat oil in frying pan and cook the capsicum, mushrooms and zucchini over medium heat for 3 minutes, or until they are soft. Cool.
2. Spread pizza bases with pasta sauce.

Top with the cooked vegetables, artichokes and corn. Sprinkle grated mozzarella on top.
3. Place on prepared trays and bake for 15–20 minutes, until cheese has melted and bases are crisp. Serve immediately.

Note: Pitta, lavash and Lebanese breads also make perfectly satisfactory bases for pizza toppings.

Sausage Rolls

Preparation time:
  20 minutes
Total cooking time:
  25 minutes
Makes 4

150 g sausage mince
1 small onion, grated
1 tablespoon barbecue
  sauce
2 tablespoons
  breadcrumbs
1 sheet ready-rolled
  puff pastry
1 egg, lightly beaten

1. Preheat oven to moderate 180°C. Line an oven tray with aluminium foil. Brush the foil with oil.

2. Combine sausage mince, onion, barbecue sauce and breadcrumbs in a medium mixing bowl. Using your hands, mix until well combined.
3. Cut the pastry sheet in half lengthways. Divide the mince mixture into two equal portions. Place one portion lengthways down the centre of each pastry sheet. Roll up and brush edges with egg to seal.
4. With seam-side down, cut each roll into two 12 cm lengths. Place on tray, bake for 25 minutes, until pastry is crisp and golden. Serve with tomato sauce.

Note: This recipe is for large sausage rolls. For a party, they can be cut into 3 cm lengths. Serve them on a tray, surrounding a bowl of tomato sauce. Or for a change, try a bottled sweet chilli sauce.

*Mini Vegetarian Pizzas (top)
and Sausage Rolls.*

Index